Sue Moules has l... in Wales... worked as a wai... ...itor currently wo... ...has been p... ...s and magazines. Her recent collections include ... *Green Seascape* and *The Earth Singing*.

The
Moth Box

Sue Moules

Parthian
The Old Surgery
Napier Street
Cardigan
SA43 1ED

www.parthianbooks.com

First published in 2013
© Sue Moules 2013
All Rights Reserved

ISBN 978-1-909844-07-0

Editor: Alan Kellermann
Cover by Alan Kellermann
Typeset by Elaine Sharples
Printed and bound by lightningsource.com

Published with the financial support of the Welsh Books Council.

British Library Cataloguing in Publication Data

A cataloguing record for this book is available from the British Library.

This book is sold subject to the condition that it shall not by way of trade or otherwise be circulated without the publisher's prior consent in any form of binding or cover other than that in which it is published.

Contents

Advantages of a Welsh Language Education	1
'A' Level	2
Welsh by Choice	4
Stations	6
Jack's Cat	8
Days Approaching The Final One	10
Traeth Gwyn, Llanina	12
In The Garden by the Orchard	14
Choosing Who Will Be the One	16
Bruges Lace Makers	17
Acorn Man	18
Love	19
Talisman	21
Zig-Zag	22
Saturday Afternoon Wedding	23
Bluebell Wood	24
The Salmon Seat	25
Learning to Kiss	26
Fireworks	27
Portmeirion in August	28
Light	29
Lobster Pots	30
In the University Library	31
Bertie's Foxgloves	32
An Email Brings the Spring	33
Cemetery	34
Seren	35
Learning the Language	36
Graffiti	37
Hay Festival	38
Individual	40
Spring Equinox	41

Storm	42
Water	43
Tracks	44
The Wood is Full of Leaves and Bird Song	45
The Starlings on the Bird Table	46
The Rookery	47
The Moth Box	48
Women for Life on Earth	49
Llyfyrgell	51
Out on the Razzle	52
Red	53
Painted	54
Potato	56
On the Subject of Identity	57
Nature Study	58
My Childhood Dolls	59
Lost Images	60
Long Ago Summers	61
By the Grinding Sea	62
Walking with Stella	63
The Leader of the Free Wales Army	64
Fences	65
Bookworm	66
The English Teachers' House	67
Acknowledgements	68

Advantages of a Welsh Language Education

She will say to you "I am Welsh English
and you are English English".

When your child is four
you make a decision.

She will come home with *Sali Mali,*
and you will learn to read phonetically.

Later you will help with homework,
and she will translate it from

one language to another with fluency,
and you will be proud.

She will say "Mummy, please don't try
and talk in Welsh; use English with my miss."

She will grow away from you
into the language of her land,

and you will be English English
and she will be Welsh.

'A' Level

When Christine's brother died
we were seventeen,
struggling
with concepts of modern theology
in that religious studies class –
a concept itself of loose construction.
Meeting
when the teacher remembered,
or was not off to Oxford for postgraduate seminars –
his weekends of lust.

Six of us knotted into concordances
and self-styled study.
Paul's journeys led us astray
through lands, cultures, modern problems.
Sixth form in that classical pillared house
relegated to spare spaces:
a converted bathroom,
ancient pipes wobbled water
through giant radiators,
worn-out desks carved
with decades of names.

When Christine's brother died
we were seventeen,
children
hiding behind a veneer of sophistication.
We left Paul writing letters of elucidation,
turned our thoughts to ethics and grief.

On Christine's return to school
we were warned of her vulnerability,
told not to say anything to upset her.

In RE classes she asked to talk
of her exclusion, of being
avoided when out shopping
as if death could be caught
on a glance.

That slow progress from coma to death,
complications of a post-mortem abroad,
papers required to fly home a coffined body.
Her brother's room as he'd left it,
child and adult, an untidy adolescent mix;
each item of identity collecting dust,
waiting his return.

Welsh by Choice

1.
You ask how I came to be here
in the land of my fathers
who are not my fathers,
in the song of the earth,
the *gwlad*, the land
where the mother calls her child.

Where I live they don't call
their children from play,
instead push them out of small houses
onto paths, parks, verges,
the spaces of childhood.

I came here long ago
into foxgloves and fireweed,
the red heart of the country,
its love of words.

Its *hiraeth*, belonging
in the land beneath our feet
that spreads to the sea,
from the sea moves inland
through lanes of goldfinches
and laburnum.

It's the dragon of the flag,
the bridge across the Severn
that makes my heart leap.

2.
I came to university
and never went home
for this was my home,
its words a clatter
opening into rivers.
"We do things differently in Wales",
someone says
chwarae teg, fair play.

My children have grown up
speaking the language,
have gone away
across the bridge.

The green of land, oldness
of language
has not held them.

I stay;
am at home.

Stations

It began on a platform smelling of earth.
A train that came through air and brittle time,
set signals at angles,
a sound in mist, a belch of steam.

Inside a carriage
on a velveteen seat, her legs dangled in air.
Above her head – framed posters,
the inevitable mirror for painting
on that red smile
before they arrived.
Under the seat,
cigarette ends ground into dirt.

Out of the windows she watched
greenery turn to factories, turn to people.
She dominated the world, looked down
into ordinary days, ordinary lives.
Women pegging washing on lines.

Back into countryside, dense and intense,
through willow-herb, scarecrows, golden corn.
Horses racing against their energy
through the field edges.

Linked with automatic doors, open plan seats,
her children sat at windows wiping dirt
into their crease-free palms.
They wriggled backwards, forwards,
confined to an egg box seat, kept asking,
"Are we getting there? Are we nearly there?"
"Soon," she said, "soon." Their friction,
 fatigue turning to tears.

"Look", colours, shapes,
buildings overshadowed their fragile lives.
The push and shove of ghetto blasters
broke through her memories.
She bundled them through Victorian exits,
down steel stairs into the dark, tired mouth
of the Underground.

Jack's Cat

A house without a cat has no soul
      Sir Patrick Moore

Sit still
but he doesn't.
He prefers to climb
the curtains,
soft paw along the bookcase,
crash down books,

to sharpen his claws
on all the door frames,
rather than the expensive
scratching post
the pet shop lady
was sure he'd use,

puts his paw in my tea;
tips over the mug,
then skitters upstairs.
Plants tumble
from the window ledge,
clatter, earth scattered.

Jumps on my lap
to chase the pen and words
across the page.
Then leaps to catch
the pattern of the wallpaper,
lanks it down in luscious curls.

I open the door,
he watches the rain,
puts out a paw,
recoils,
turns back indoors,
settles in the best chair.

Days Approaching the Final One

Spring flings its exuberance
against the strong window.
She sits in an easy chair indoors,
looks out at us
and trees
birthing their leaves.

In the warm, surrounded
by photos of pasts: weddings,
children, grandchildren.
Asked how she feels, is not deceived
by our brash contempt of death,
our strange deceit and bright chat,
replies "still doddering on, lingering here".

We treat her as if she cannot know,
elide truth from sentences,
show positivity in everything.
Behind dark evening blinds
and snooker on the box,
she knows this is the last winter.

We are all standing stones,
isolated and lonely.
Decay, sleep, rest,
there's no way to prepare us.
She keeps kitchen contents
to bare necessities:
a waiting spell
for us to accept departure.

Spring notches its fresh shoots
in winter ground,
days pass,
still we string sophistry.

Daffodils blow sunlight
edging our grief.

Traeth Gwyn, Llanina

Once we'd take the footpath
through St Ina's churchyard.
Now the path is through the wood,
where the river Llethi runs to the sea.

In the churchyard, the grave
of poet and campaigner Dot Clancy,
dancing shoes and words.
Her funeral overflowing, a trumpeter played
When the Saints go Marching in.

We cross the river
on the wedge of stone and wire,
up steps to the lookout point,
and down to the sea.

Smugglers unloaded booty,
took it up through the church into the woods.
From here Dylan Thomas walked into New Quay
composing sentences in his head.

Dogs race around.
Warm sand on our feet,
sea lapping our ankles.

From driftwood, abandoned rope,
plastic shoes,
fish boxes, broken bouys
we sculpt a land-locked boat.

"This is my favourite place", my son says,
"The Pirate Beach".

In the Garden by the Orchard

In the spring light of the garden –
fresh green of new leaf –
the lovers meet.
He watches her,
hidden by the welter of leaves.
She doesn't see him.

Light wisps her hair into a halo,
her face sculpted in sun
as she gathers flowers in her basket.
He walks in on her reverie
as she stoops and rises.
Trees shade them,
bird song filters through
as new leaves and darker ones merge.

They have
aged into the couple
who sit together,
remember those two people
they once were.
The garden holds them:
he grows vegetables,
she, mists of flowers.

Each year that miracle
turns bare trees into fountains of green,
cascades of birds.
Buds burst into leaf, shatter the landscape
with their fecundity
in the spring of the garden.

Choosing Who Will Be the One

One potato, two,
in our playground games
three potato, four,
this root we live on
five potato, six,
from Peru, first cultivated
ten thousand years ago,
seven potato, more.

We chanted the words,
oblivious of history
and the failure of the potato.
Our fists held out
to be part of the game.
Our bags of crisps
waiting for later.

Bruges Lace Makers

Grandmothers sat outside,
straw-stuffed pillows on their laps
weaving ancient patterns.

These dowagers, a cottage industry.
They put out their hands:
coins for a photo.

Their bobbins, thin bagpipes,
thread over each other as they plaited
fine filigree into lace.

It's lace that's brought us here,
the way yarn can weave
its ancient skill into art.

Acorn Man

for Jim Crace

A pruning knife
in one of your father's pockets,
the other full of acorns.

He heeled acorns
into empty spaces of land.

Now trees flourish,
lift fronded arms
to hold bird song.

To have a pocket of acorns
is to have childhood.
We are blessed
with people
who take the simple seed
and make the future.

In each tree your father's memory;
he is there in each new leaf.
In the autumn
as cups of acorns fall
others gather pocketfuls,
heel them into wasteland.

Love

The heart is always involved.
Not those hearts and flowers
found on cards in February,
but the life-muscle.

We used to write *luv*.
It wasn't the same as love –
the old-fashioned kind –
but what was love?
Could it be weighed out and analysed?

For some it was an everyday word
yes love, no love,
my lovely, my lover.
For others love was sacred,
reserved for Sunday
and the cold stone of church
where love was proclaimed
in carved letters.
It was those large families –
a child every year,
the older ones pushing the pram.

Underneath all our lives
there is love,
that unbearable hug
that won't let us go.

Love's like that –
is there and gone –
quick as a clock,
it speeds by,
leaves us waiting.

Talisman

Peacocks dance an exotic shiver of feathers,
fanned out and quivered
tail of eyes watching,
a panoply of blue-green shimmer.
Later see the train dragged around,
a trail of fabric,
eyes squashed in mud.

There at Tŷ Hen all those years ago,
then along the stone wall in Gorrig,
in the castle grounds at Cardiff.

A feather for luck.
I tassle the barbs to the indigo eye
re-smooth the turquoise elegance,
place the feather in a drawer
with the coin in the cork,
the four leaf clover you found –
touchstones for luck.

I should throw them out,
but I won't.

Zig-Zag

for Mary MacGregor

There are no stars tonight
as we walk into the dark
from the light of the bookshop
talking about words and time.

"I love the Welsh word for time,
amser," you say
breaking it down
into *am* and *ser* –
around stars.
You quote Dylan Thomas:
"And time has ticked a heaven round the stars"
writing *amser* in the margin
of his poem.

You are a face at poetry readings,
a lover of words,
you tell me another favourite:
igam-ogam, for zig-zag.

Time parts us in the car park,

I take with me words like stars
to light my zig-zag way.

Saturday Afternoon Wedding

On the bench
that looks out at the road,
a child dangles her legs
to the sound of the church bells
tumbling their wedding peal.

A bird sings.
An orange digger on a truck
and a stream of grey cars
drive into the town.

They pass the quiet doctors' surgery,
the shut chemist,
the closed newsagent,
the flower shop
with its trays of winter pansies and violas.

All on the conveyor belt road
with somewhere to go,
and in a freeze-frame of bride and groom
the bells trill.

Bluebell Wood

I walk for indigo perfume –
amble tree-rooted paths, hear the river
in the green of the earthy room.

In the rhythm of the gloom
where new light and new leaves quiver
in this woodland where I walk for indigo perfume,

hear the chiffchaff, and know that soon
the trees will be full of song and fervour
in the green of the earthy room

where ancient bulbs still bloom
in the cascade of carpet that gives
this woodland where I walk for indigo perfume,

and find there spring in full tune:
warblers and cuckoos echo the river
in the green of the earthy room.

Even at night by the light of the moon,
the closed flowers are a fragrant cover
in the woodland where I walk for indigo perfume,
in the green of the earthy room.

The Salmon Seat

Over the bridge
and down by the Teifi,
where boulders
constrict the bounce of water,
the river sounds
strong in its song.

The salmon bench has gone,
broken,
but the wood carved fish
are still here, sculptures now.

No salmon or canoeists today
just the river rush.

A man greets me:
"Mae hi'n braf", he says,
and from a lost well

"Ydy, wir", I reply,
that sound
like the river

deep.

Learning to Kiss

Not like the kisses aunts gave
with lipstick and powder mark,
which I rubbed off,
or the kiss I had to offer
on their papery skin.

My first kiss was to a pillow:
pucker up the lips,
press into the cotton pillowcase,
and practise
like playing the trombone –
make a heart shape,
let it open into the little *pp*
or the longer *ppp*,
lips on lips held fast at the breath,

the pillow with its clean scent
and no response.

Fireworks

Jumping Jacks, bangers,
red and green flare matches,
sparklers, golden rain, rockets,
silver fountains, Catherine Wheels –
they sounded like sweets.
We'd buy a selection box,
open the tissue paper
to the acrid smell of danger.

After the dahlia season
the flower beds were a tumble
of frosted, fallow earth.
We'd stand in woolly hats and gloves
by the kitchen door,
sparklers burning the air,
illuminating our faces
as we spun our names.

My father set up the display in the garden.
From milk bottles he'd launch rockets,
a whirr through the November night – *bang* –
a cascade of stars.
Golden rain's explosion, a fountain of glitter.
The sudden jump of bangers
out of their cardboard cylinders.

Before our jacket potatoes,
the Catherine Wheel,
her body circling on a nail,
a crucifixion of sparks.

Portmeirion in August

Blue stars dazzle the foliage,
pink mixes with blue –
a regatta of indigo hydrangeas.
Last time we were here, spring was
vivid with rhododendrons.

Hydrangeas are delicate spirals,
light spindles of fantasy
in a garden of make believe;
a landlocked boat, a balcony of sea.

A lake silver-transparent
where carp flick edges,
curve the lily pads.
A squirrel sunbathes on a picnic table,
oblivious to tourists.

In Y Gwyllt, slated woodland,
through monkey trails
of rhododendron leaves,
thick trunks, light and shade
entwine in a thicket.

We climb higher to the dogs' cemetery,
a ghost garden.
Down in the village
a tower struts, a dome preens
in the sway of flowers.

Light

To wake early in pink light
as day opens.

On the horizon the cattle
gleam in the stained glass.

The sky breaks through,
blue solid on purple,

grass, hills,
the farm's milking parlour.

Always a rush,
uniforms, PE kit, packed lunches.

The way we drive away
into ordinary things.

Lobster Pots

We photograph their negative space,
the rope structures tarred black
to keep the sea from eating through.
The crabs and lobsters see nothing;
blunder in from deep dark.

Out here on the sea wall
with the smell of fish and diesel
they are empty hives
against the green and white of fishing boats
Lady Jane, Emily, Princess,
brisk sea air,
sky so blue it looks painted.

Tonight in the deep
these shapes will hold sea.

In the University Library

I'm in the library again,
warm, surrounded by books.

Outside on the hockey pitch
The Sealed Knot are marching
in a row of red and black shields:
"step, step, step, step, stop".
A wall of warriors, they wield their spears.

I pull myself back from the window
to the book and words.
Over thirty years ago
I sat here looking at words,
and I'm here again as if it was then,
in between
a gallop of lost time.

I look up, away from the words
and out into the cold,
see the hockey team practise,
seagulls waddle over the pitch.
Move back from then, a time of memory,
to civil war battles,
a Friday afternoon now.

Bertie's Foxgloves

On the wall outside his house
Bertie nurtures digitalis seedlings.
Sun shocks their soft leaves,
the muscle strength
of this heart flower.

Slugs know about its deadly sap
and keep away.

He gives me a clump
for my garden.
I'll wait two years
for their variegated bells,
an aura of purple
and white light,
their seed-stars.

An Email Brings the Spring

A chiffchaff warbles on your morning walk
and ten other birds in song,
Spring is almost sprung.

The daffodils nearly
ready to break through their green
to let out sunshine.

Crocus on the lawn open their beaks,
trees shake catkins,
lambs in the brown fields.

And to crack the frost
that rinds these March mornings
the wren is singing.

Cemetery

There must be nine hundred people here, facing East.
I am not frightened
as I walk through dawn's purple light,
along pews of time, a theatre of names:
Sarah Morgan, Gethin Williams, Jonah Jones,
Rachel Davies, our beloved son Thomas.

Surprised that so many can be neatly arranged
in an acre of land bordered by grazing cows,
a council estate, the awesome valley of church.
Children's voices rise from Ysgol Ffynnonbedr
as they run, blue and grey
through the playground's chill.

They learn the past from books,
but their register of names is little changed
from those residing under clay and slate
in neat lines on the slope of hill
patiently waiting its increase.

Seren

January's forest snow crunches under footsteps.
Stars glisten;
a heaven pitted with jewels.

Loneliness has crept into our lives,
has found a touchstone in friendship,
a togetherness that radiates as we walk,
our hands and heads gloved in wool.

"What is star in Welsh?" I ask.
Seren.
We crush reflections in evening's
white, silent space.

Learning the Language

Still I can't speak it
although I can understand
if you don't talk too fast
and run words together
like a necklace of sound.

"Siaradwch yn araf"
"Speak slowly please"
"I understand, but am not fluent"
I can say my name
and where I live,
but I stumble at the mutations.

Just when I'm confident
the language changes
this way and that.
I'm lost again,
drowning in words.

Graffiti

Houses fill with fish
in a reservoir once a village.
In drought years,
tombs in the cemetery
break through.

"Cofiwch Dryweryn"
painted on a derelict cottage
by a poet in protest.
The National Trust
has bought the property –
sixties graffiti is history.

A North Wales village
where water is piped to England.
In hot summers the rubble roof tops
of Capel Celyn reveal the truth,
drowned memories of a people
in the sea of Cantre Gwaelod.

Hay Festival

Imagine this:
people queue,
spilling over walkways,
wait to hear poetry.

The marquee is full,
it's hot and yet everyone
sits there intent,
listening to poetry.

The queue for the book-signing
folds and re-folds,
a maze of people
standing, reading poetry.

The new book is sold out.
"We ordered 1,500 copies"
says the bookseller
"and they've all gone".

Two hours later:
 the poets are still signing,
"surely they'll stop – we'll be turned away"
someone says.

We move along
up to the poets
who still have time to chat,
sign our books with kisses.

I am not imaging this.
It happened
a day in a field
where the earth is red.

Individual

Not even a twin
can have the same finger prints
whorled into hands.

The patterns of skin
we shed and re-grow
like the iris aura of eyes –
ours, and ours alone.

Spring Equinox

A quarter way through
and the year warms:
daffodils, bird song,
brighter mornings,
longer evenings.
Beech leaves unfurl,
fresh green.

Holy days
and the Pagan moon
resurrect light.
Rabbits, hares,
bluebells, gorse –
earth's re-birth.

Storm

The wind rises, knocks against windows,
tangles the trees.
Rain batters down against her face
as she hurries home
along the tumble of pavement,
the swirl of rushing leaves.

She slams the door,
glad to be out of the sting of wind,
the soak of rain.
The sky grumbles, turns dark
as she puts on the light;
it stutters and goes out.

Wind lifts the catch from the gate,
bangs it along its hinges,
leaves it to clatter back and forth.
She finds a candle, sits in the dark room
listening to the belch of wind and rain
as it slatters the house.

Water

tumbles over rocks,
a harp of silk,

twists and curves
along narrow rivers,

muscles its skein of power,

punches its current
into eddies and whirlpools;
white swirls of danger,

chunders in and out,
a roar of ocean edging beaches
with breakers of foam,

keeps its power hidden,
a caged animal
ready to leap barriers,
drown towns.

Tracks

The cat's pink paws
make patterns
in the snow,
crunch and crackle
as he dances his shadow.

We walk through snow,
making our mark
over other footprints
and tyre tracks.

The world is transformed,
and we are confined
by the expanse of white,
the steps we take
to mark our way.

The Wood is Full of Leaves and Bird Song

Shamrocks of wood sorrel, bluebell leaves fountain,
hold up thick stems of fragrant bells.

Buds unfurl over branches. Season of the leaf:
from newborn green to dark maturity.

A scatter of light through leaves
spangles along the path's aisle.
Shades and tones merge

in the wood where
birds coo and warble
under the echo of *'cuckoo'*.

The Starlings on the Bird Table

They glisten in their newly combed outfits,
preen their polka dots,
squabble like children.
It's not fair, it's not fair
as they stab their beaks
into carrot cake, roast potatoes.

They tip food over the ledge,
scatter crocuses with remnants
for the timid sparrows and blue-tits.
The starlings tug-of-war the food,
bicker, an unsettled schoolroom.

They make so much noise
I leave my breakfast, lift the net curtain
and check there is no cat about.
The brylcreemed birds lift as arrows.

The Rookery

Most of the horse-chestnut trees have gone;
the space marked out
as parking bays.
No rooks,
a solitary magpie
pecking
at the rubbish left
by the twice-yearly fair.
The ancient rite of colour and noise.

The rooks have left,
moved across town to a quieter car park
where ancient hazels susurrate
their heavy twig nests
with a lace of green light.

Here a gossip of rooks
fill the air with their chatter,
black shadows pecking
cartons inside out.
Their loud rant
startles the plain song
of the smaller birds.

At night a cacophony
wobbles the tree tops
as the birds settle above our heads.

The Moth Box

We have caught the night.
It sleeps in here,
pulled in by light.

We open it in day,
take out the shapes
and name them.

Scorched Wing, Tussock,
White Ermine, Marbled Coronet,
Green Carpet, Phoenix.

We lift them out,
look at them through hand lenses,
marvel at their intricacy.

We leave them in the shade
to sleep out;
they merge into garden.

Later, they will flap in quick quivers,
heat their delicate tiled wings,
soar into the dark.

Women for Life on Earth

THEN

At Greenham Common,
I was there because I was a woman,
because I got on the coach;
left Wales for Newbury.

I was there in cold winter weather,
scared at the razor wire, waves
of barbs braided over concrete posts.

The strong link fence
tied with ribbons and mementos:
children's shoes and teddy bears.
Beyond, the American soldiers
patrolled the nuclear bunker.

A weekend trying to sleep
in a damp tent; our presence the protest.
I got back on the coach,
slept all the way home.

NOW

The wood is just a wood,
the wire fence pulled down,
the bunker removed.

Those banshee screams
of unleashed women
and the cold wind
are almost a myth.

Yet the *out, out, out*
still shouts through the trees

still echoes.

Llyfyrgell

In Welsh class
our Saxon tongues stumble
over this word, *library*.
We use another language,
call it *bibliotheque,*
as our tongues can manage that.

Inside the cell of books
words are folded into covers.
Contained, catalogued, tamed.
A row of computers
the way forward;
no more pages to stale with time.

But these words can't be borrowed.
Won't fit in your bag;
take you home on the bus
in a different world.

Out on the Razzle

My doppelgänger
has been out again,
putting me in places
I'm not usually seen.
Last night I was pub crawling
down the High Street
singing loudly, out of tune.

When I complain
that actually I was at home
watching *Eastenders,* eating up
the last of the Christmas chocolate,
no one believes me,
because I was seen
or my ghost was seen
painting the town red.

Red

The colour of Christmas,
warmth and fire,
of Valentine's day and hearts.

Such wonderful names
for its shades:
scarlet, vermillion, crimson
all the tones of sunrise and sunset.
It is blood and life.

It is the Chinese New Year;
luck and expectation.
Such a positive colour.

Yet I don't like it.

I make myself wear it
to ground myself
in its base colour
and something happens –
people say
that red dress suits you,
I'm warmed by the glow.

Painted

How many hearts and flowers
can you have needled into your flesh?
Discreet of course,
on buttock, breast
or the bottom of the spine
seen only by those you love,
or everyone in communal changing rooms.

Made in 1986 said one
as she stepped
into her almost not there bikini.
Another displayed a rose,
delicate as watercolour.
One had her whole body
as a picture of Celtic swirls,
a rainbow down her back.

If younger would I consider one?
No, the pain of the needle
and permanence would put me off.
Yet as a child, I'd cover my arms
with transfers, wet blobs of paper
painted my skin with a gallery.

A bleed of navy and green ink
on the bulging arm muscles
of the men who smoked Players
or Craven A in my father's shop.
Unshaved faces and rough language
as they held out their oil-stained palms
for me to take the money,
ink from their newspapers
patterning my hands.

I look at my hands
and would have them
hennaed with exotic swirls,
elegant, a siren in the making.
But not a tattoo,
a scar, a memory.
a number worried under skin.

Potato

I worry the word's staccato –
potato from *patata* –
into the starch of my being.

I don't like potatoes much.
I tolerate their versatility,
their easy carbohydrate.

They've been here
for five hundred years,
coming from Spain on Raleigh's ship.

Nightshade leaves, small stars, flowers
that triumph in tuber coins.
Even I can grow them.

Don't plant them in the same place twice,
blight can attack the crop,
send their leaves black.

It brought starvation –
a whole country unearthed.

On the Subject of Identity

This is only half the picture.
The other me is someone else
sunning on a beach,
or being taken out to dinner.

I'm just the negative, the shape
from which she was cut.

I watch the other me.
She doesn't look behind or inside
to the shadow that shouts
you can't do this!

Nature Study

That text book
with pen and ink illustrations of flowers.
Stamen, stigma, anther,
the amazing seeds of grasses.
She tried to draw them,
learn their Latin names.

Each day she went walking –
her boots covered with seeds
of fescue and timothy –
she gathered pine cones,
rosehips, the feather of a magpie
with its glisten of jade.

If she'd not been so squeamish,
had dissected the frog,
but remembered
that tray of dead amphibians,
scalpels and the smell of formaldehyde.
It had taken her away from nature.

My Childhood Dolls

That brief time of the bride doll
perfect in her white lace,
complete with shoes and veil.
She didn't want to take it out of the box.

Nothing could replace brittle plastic Anna,
her large head mended with UHU glue
to seal the crack in her moulded hair.

Anna went everywhere with her
until the day she disappeared.

Lost Images

Old age has scorched his eyes,
left the retina imageless.
Taken words from his fingers,
numbers from his watch.

The paper is read to him,
he has to ask the time,
and could you dial the digits
so he can make a phone call?

He can't write a cheque,
distinguish between a £5 and £10 note,
the seed packets he ordered lie dormant.
reading and driving are past tense.

The retina is worn out,
images, burnt paper.

Long Ago Summers

The boats in the harbour,
siesta afternoons,
the dusty buzz of early evening
with its hum of things about to happen,
the tang of food in the air.

The harbour noise,
fishermen at their nets,
seagulls scuttering sky,
fish crates of silver scales,
the smell of brine and fish.

The charm of shopping,
wandering in boulevards
for floating stars of chiffon dresses,
then a rest on a park bench
to watch the ritual walking of poodles.

Those long hot nights,
the wrap of arms round my body,
sea's slow lap
as the moon gradually drowned.

By the Grinding Sea

after Dylan Thomas

The sea erodes the cliffs,
tumbles their minerals into sand.
Here we find fossils of glass,
rubbish taken out to sea,
broken down and returned as treasure
among mussel and razor shells.

The sea grinds our memories,
condenses them into sand.
We try to gather them,
but the colours mix
into nebulous grey.

Walking with Stella

We turn where the cows have lumbered,
trek through the gluck of mud.
Past the blackthorn,
a skein of geese trumpet the sky.

On the beach the old blue-planked boat,
overtaken with saffron gorse.
All our walks cross this sand and shale;
birds we can't name scutter over stones.

We turn our backs on the sea,
go through the gate. Along the footpath
a trundle of violets splash their indigo
from verge and stone wall.

We walk over the railway line,
see the two-carriage train
rumble into the distance,
the rails still hot with its song.

On and past the wood
where the bluebells are still white,
we hear the drill, stop, drill, stop
of a woodpecker hidden in trees.

The Leader of the Free Wales Army

You'd find Cayo Evans in the *Ivy Bush*
drinking with farmers and students.
In his worn black leather jacket
he thought he was James Dean.

At his *Glan Denys* mansion
a room of guns.
In the fields, his mares and foals
nuzzled the edges of the fence.

His mother collected rent
from students who lived in the flats.
Cayo emptied the electric meters
after visits from his ex-wife.

On hay-scented evenings
Jock played the accordion,
the men drank beer,
shot empty cans off the wall.

Dusk fell slowly to the music,
while the fields swayed
with the movement of horses
undulating like the hills.

Fences

Between my front garden and theirs
a hedge of rugosa, tethered stems and spikes.
A tangle of green, ready to draw blood.
In the morning, the new growth
rosters in sunlight, pink petals open,
for bees to make the rose hips.
I will scissor off in autumn, simmer into syrup.

I ask if I might prune back the foliage
that casts darkness over my lupins.
"Yeh" you say, "we're not into gardening,"
as your dandelions dazzle
with their parachute display.
So I clip the brambles
that dig through my gardeners' gloves,
cleave their teasel into my flesh.

In the back garden
the shiplap panels of faded creosote
left by the previous tenant
are flimsy where the young Alsatian
jumps up and rests his weight.
Every gale lifts the fence a little more,
and on either side we stake the supports
in the wet dark, to keep our separateness.

Bookworm

for Dawn

This small bookshop
is packed with stories.
People congregate among words,
safe among printed pages,
browse, chat, buy.

Treasure on the shelves
where words are stored,
their inside covers priced in pencil.

Some only want pre-loved books –
not the new ones in the window,
but a dialogue with hands and hearts
who have read these pages before.

Trees opposite sway in the wind,
the old brown clock turns time around.

The English Teachers' House

They spoke in iambic pentameter:
will you please pass the sugar bowl and spoon.
Beyond the politeness, their heads
were in other lands and places,

with Beowulf, or Gawain in search
of the Green Knight, or on the road
to Canterbury with Chaucer
and his story-telling pilgrims.

They read *The Guardian*, knew a million
different things, but couldn't remember
where they'd left their long distance glasses.
One would start a sentence, the other finish it.

Their love was tangled up in the history
of words on their bookcases.
In bed at night, snake-entwined,
they'd ask each other to define passion.

Acknowledgements

Acknowledgements are due to the following magazines and anthologies in which some of these poems first appeared:

Ambit, New Welsh Review, Poetry Wales, Staple, The Interpreter's House, The Western Mail, The Visitors Anthology (Cinnamon), The Listening Shell Anthology (Headland), Yorkshire Open Poetry Competition Anthology, 1989, *This Global Warming: Awel Aman Tawe Competition Anthology.*

I am grateful to Teifi Writers for the commission to write the poem 'Welsh by Choice'.

Lightning Source UK Ltd.
Milton Keynes UK
UKOW04f1339061013

218541UK00001B/3/P